D0656126

KINGDOM LIFE

THE FOUNDATION SERIES

The Foundations series, published in association with the Evangelical Alliance, covers aspects of everyday life and faith crucial to today's Christian. Each book addresses a different theme and defines what evangelical Christians believe and why. Topics include the Bible, evangelism, prayer, guidance, evangelicalism and miracles.

'Thought-provoking and faith-building, this series of Christian basics should be read widely.' *Clive Calver*

KINGDOM LIFE

Martin Goldsmith

HODDER AND STOUGHTON
LONDON SYDNEY AUCKLAND TORONTO

British Library Cataloguing in Publication Data

Goldsmith, Martin, *1934*–
Kingdom life.
1. Bible. N.T. Special subjects. Christian doctrine. Kingdom of God
I. Title
231.7′2

ISBN 0 340 42634 9

Copyright © 1988 by Martin Goldsmith. First printed 1988. All rights reserved. No part of this publication may be reproduced or transmitted in any form or by any means, electronically or mechanically, including photocopying, recording or any information storage or retrieval system, without either the prior permission in writing from the publisher or a licence, permitting restricted copying. In the United Kingdom such licences are issued by the Copyright Licensing Agency, 33–34 Alfred Place, London WC1E 7DP. *Printed in Great Britain for Hodder and Stoughton Limited, Mill Road, Dunton Green, Sevenoaks, Kent by Cox and Wyman Limited, Reading, Berks. Photoset by Rowland Phototypesetting Limited, Bury St Edmunds, Suffolk. Hodder and Stoughton Editorial Office: 47 Bedford Square, London WC1B 3DP.*

To Elizabeth
my much-loved wife
and joyful companion,
unfailing in her encouragement,
gentle in her criticisms,
a perceptive editor.

CONTENTS

FOREWORD

The modern reader of the New Testament may be surprised to find John the Baptist and Jesus starting their preached message with the announcement that 'the kingdom of heaven is at hand' (Matt. 3:2; 4:17) without any explanation of what they mean by the expression 'kingdom of heaven'. Clearly they assumed a widespread knowledge of the traditional Jewish understanding of the kingdom.

Christians today lack that background of rabbinic teaching, so we easily fall into wrong ideas about the life of the kingdom. While there are various solid theological works to guide the expert on this subject, it seems that we need careful biblical expositions of the kingdom in popular form, for we are assailed by the left and right wings of evangelicalism on this topic.

Is the kingdom life particularly evidenced by signs and wonders plus vibrant worship and close-knit church life? Or is 'the kingdom' shorthand for a passionate concern for social justice? Or is it intimately connected to repentance and holiness with humility?

How did Jesus and John the Baptist picture the kingdom life?

These burning issues are hot potatoes in the church today. They are also central to the message of the New Testament itself. The gospels and the teaching of Jesus are based on the message of the kingdom. The epistles continue to some extent that central teaching of kingdom life, but concentrate more on the king of the kingdom, Jesus Christ himself. He is Lord of all. In any biblical Christian teaching and in all true kingdom living Jesus Christ our Lord must be centre-stage. In this book we shall attempt to examine some of these fundamental questions about the kingdom, but we must not allow our quest for kingdom life to displace the person and work of Jesus Christ from his central position. Let him be praised, honoured, served and loved!

1

THE KINGDOM

'Repent, for the kingdom of heaven is at hand' (Matt. 3:2). Dressed in camel skins and eating only locusts and wild honey, John the Baptist burst on to the stage of history. He flouted all the fads of fashion, but people flocked out from the city into the wilderness to hear his message. Among the crowds was Jesus himself, who then began his ministry with the same words – 'Repent, for the kingdom of heaven is at hand' (Matt. 4:17).

To all outward appearances Jesus was just like all the others in the crowd, but actually this was the King of kings breaking into world history to inaugurate the kingdom of God on earth. As we shall see, this would contrast sharply with the world's values: God's rule is radical, with its totally different goals and lifestyle.

At first Jesus did not explain what he meant by 'the kingdom of God'. In the coming months he would fill in many of the details of his vision. But he was also aware that his audience had considerable background understanding of the kingdom from their knowledge of the Old Testament and the traditional teaching of the rabbis.

The Jews had such rich experience of God as king. Life as slaves in Egypt was hopeless and demoralising – and then God had stepped in to deliver them from the might of Pharaoh. He overwhelmed the Egyptians with his amazing miracles and finally slaughtered all the first-born babies in Egypt. Pharaoh was quick to let them go after that! Then the Egyptian army chased Israel to bring them back into slavery. But God drowned the lot in the Red Sea. He marched in a pillar of cloud and fire before the Israelites (the kings of the surrounding nations also marched at the head of their people). Like the kings of other nearby peoples God also encamped right in their midst. He provided for them all they needed as they journeyed through the interminable barren wilderness, finally bringing them joyfully across the river Jordan into the promised land.

The divine king is always gracious and mighty. Now, as the crowds listened to Jesus, they wondered, 'Will God still do such things for his people? In ruling over us, will he deliver us, give us victory, dwell in our midst, provide for us, bring us safely into the promised new heaven and new earth?'

But years ago, after some time in the promised land their forefathers had demanded, 'appoint for us a king to govern us like all the nations' (1 Sam. 8:5). What a fearful request from a people who had known *God* as their king! It was a treacherous and rebellious decision to choose a mere human king to rule over them. No wonder God said to Samuel, 'they have rejected me from being king over them' (1 Sam. 8:7). In their desire for authoritative human leadership like the surrounding heathen nations they turned their backs on the kingly rule of God. Saul, David and the other kings were poor substitutes for God as king.

In the Old Testament it is clear too that God not only rules over his own people Israel but also over all the nations. Pharaoh, Nebuchadnezzar, Cyrus and others thought they had power. Pride can easily go to the head of powerful world leaders! But actually God rules over them all, determining the rise and fall of empires. He also judges the nations for their sins, so the prophets have long chapters declaring 'woe' to Edom, Moab and others.

Memories of their past history will have raced through the minds of the listening crowds when they heard both John and Jesus preaching about the kingdom of God. What John introduced, Jesus takes much further.

He elaborates the theme of the kingdom particularly in the Sermon on the Mount

(Matt. 5–7), shattering normal ideas of how to run a society. His ideals seem impossible. This radical sermon starts with the so-called Beatitudes. These begin and end with the kingdom. Who are the key men in the kingdom of God? Men of powerful faith? Religious leaders? No! The poor in spirit and the meek, those who mourn and who hunger and thirst for righteousness, the merciful, the pure in heart, the peacemakers and those who are persecuted for righteousness' sake and for Jesus.

Jesus' teaching on kingdom life still shocks us today.

'Tremendous worship!' 'A wonderful time of prayer!' 'Brilliant fellowship!' 'Lord, Lord, we love you.' Jesus pulls us up short by saying that such things are not the true life of the kingdom. The kingdom, he says, is not found in pious people saying 'Lord, Lord' or in 'religious' experiences but in obediently doing the will of God the Father (Matt. 7:21). Such obedience is the rock-like foundation for a true kingdom life; everything else is unstable sand (Matt. 7:24–27). Kingdom life will not be seen in how we worship, but in whether we hear Jesus' words and do them (Matt. 7:24). This is God's purpose for all those who recognise Jesus as king and enter his kingdom. It is not surprising that we read that the crowds were astonished at Jesus' teaching (Matt. 7:28). It is radical!

Some Christians today feel it is right to present a brutally clear message of the gospel. Jesus was not like that. Understanding that people needed help to grasp the new values, he used parables for everyday life so that those with spiritually open ears would hear, but the hard of heart would not understand. To grasp the secrets of the kingdom is a spiritual gift (Matt. 13:11). To those whose ears and eyes are opened, more will be given in the continuously growing life of the kingdom (Matt. 13:12).

The kingdom parables

The sower (Matt. 13:3–8, 18–23; Mk. 4:3–8, 14–20)
Every Sunday school child knows this story of the seed that fell on the path, on rocky ground, among thorns and in good soil. The seed is the message of the kingdom. Some hearers are so hard-hearted that the word has no entry into their minds or hearts. Some receive it joyfully but lack the perseverance to endure through times of persecution or difficulty. Others receive the word, but it proves unfruitful because of their 'delight in riches' (Mk. 4:19). We cannot grow in the kingdom life when 'the cares of the world' (Mk. 4:19) rival the Lord for supremacy in our lives. God longs for those who will 'hear the word and understand it'

(Matt. 13:23) – we notice here the importance of the spoken word (not just visible signs) and our intelligent use of the mind to grasp its meaning. In this way we shall bear fruit – some more, some less, but God is equally pleased with the hundredfold, sixtyfold and thirtyfold – he is looking for us to fulfil our potential and for fruit-bearing growth in our lives.

The harvest (Matt. 13:24–30; Mk. 4:26–29)
Matthew tells the story of a man who sows good seed in his field, but then an enemy comes at night and sows weeds there too. Both the wheat and the weeds grow together in the field. The owner refuses to allow his servants to try and remove the weeds lest they damage the true seed. Only at the final harvest will they be separated. Then the weeds will be burnt and the wheat gathered into the master's barn.

The emphasis in this story is on our need to wait for the final harvest. The judgement of the kingdom will not be apparent until the final judgement day. Until then the true and the false grow together in the kingdom. How true that is of the church! Many long to weed out the unspiritual from the church and develop a single-minded church consisting only of like-minded spiritual men and women. This parable shatters that sort of dream. In rooting out the weeds we shall damage some of the true believers, for our handling of people is never totally sensitive and discerning. We may even think that some of the true stalks of wheat are just weeds! So be patient with the church of God!

Mark's equivalent story is somewhat different. His emphasis is that the kingdom of God is like seed which grows without human effort. We merely see the growth of the seed and enjoy the end result in the harvest. So often a true work of the kingdom flourishes quite apart from our endeavours. There is something sovereignly mysterious about the working of God. We love to try to analyse the causes – 'Was it because people prayed or because evangelism became a priority or because . . . ? Actually it was entirely due to God himself! Let us enjoy his working and gather in the harvest as he prepares it for us.

Mustard seed and leaven (Matt. 13:31–33; Mk. 4:30–32; Lk. 13:18–21)
The tiny mustard seed becomes a mighty shrub. The leaven causes the bread to rise and become a significant loaf. The kingdom seems small and unimportant, but it grows. Jesus started as a small baby, but grew (Lk. 2:52). The church too started very small and only among Jewish people, but became gradually a large international movement. Each of us individually starts in the kingdom with new birth, but must grow in Christ until we enter the glory of being perfectly like our Lord.

From these two parables we learn not only that the kingdom grows, but also that we must not despise what is tiny and apparently insignificant. We love to boast of big churches and meetings. We are tempted to judge on the basis of statistics. But God may surprise us by making a tiny bit of leaven influence the growth of the whole church. A minuscule seed may become the great tree.

It should also be noted how the birds of the air find shade beneath the branches of that tree. From early times it was understood that the birds here represent the nations of the earth. Later we shall again note how the kingdom of God is for all nations. The tree of the kingdom was not just to give shelter to Jewish birds, but to all peoples.

Treasure and pearl (Matt. 13:44–46)
A farmer finds treasure in a field. A merchant finds a priceless pearl. Both sell all they have in order to buy it. The kingdom of God is of such immense value that it is worth sacrificing everything we have in order to enjoy it. To be totally under God's gracious rule is the secret of all joy in life. Only with the Lord do our lives have their true value and worth. When we come to the Lord for his life-giving salvation we surrender all we have and all we are to his control. So it was that the early church's baptismal creed was 'Jesus is Lord'. Jesus becomes our boss in every detail of life.

Many people fear the cost of becoming a follower of Jesus. They realise they may have to give up a girl or boy friend. They wonder what it will mean for their professional career. Will he push them into missionary work or into some other form of ministry? Will they become religious cranks and lose all their friends? They need not be anxious. The glories of Jesus Christ are worth any sacrifice and God loves us so much that he does not want to spoil our lives. He will enrich them beyond compare.

Good and bad fish (Matt. 13:47–50)
Just as the wheat and tares grow together in the kingdom, so also now the fishing net gathers in fish of every kind, both good and bad. This little parable again stresses the final judgement when God will 'separate the evil from the righteous, and throw them into the furnace of fire' (Matt. 13:49). It is not popular today to preach about heaven and hell. We prefer to talk about the blessings of the Christian life here on earth. But the New Testament has much to say about our ultimate future. It not only gives us the promise of an assured hope if we are true followers of Jesus Christ, but it also warns of 'the furnace of fire' where 'men will weep and gnash their teeth' (Matt. 13:50). It is good for us to be reminded of the final judgement which is the climax of the kingdom. The glories of eternal life with

our beloved Jesus Christ encourage us to persevere even through hard times. The threat of damnation warns us not to play games with the living God. It alerts us too to the urgent need to share the good news of salvation in Christ with men and women all over the world.

Summary

So we see that the term 'kingdom' is rich and wide in its significance, covering many facets of God's gracious working in the world and for his people.

'The kingdom of God implies the whole of the preaching of Jesus Christ and his apostles,' says one commentator; another defines the kingdom of God as 'the basic theme which Jesus proclaimed, the core or essence of his teaching'; some rabbis described the kingdom of God as the very truth or essence of the law. The idea of the kingdom is virtually equivalent to the whole gospel. It has been said that the words 'kingdom', 'salvation' and 'eternal life' are almost interchangeable. In submission to God as king we find salvation and the assurance of eternal life. Certainly Matthew refers frequently to the gospel of the kingdom as the basis of the preached message (Matt. 4:23; 9:35; 10:7; 13:19; 24:14) and in Acts too Jesus and the apostles preach the kingdom of God (Acts 1:3; 8:12; 19:8; 20:25; 28:23, 31). Preaching Jesus, preaching the gospel and preaching the kingdom are just different ways of saying the same thing.

To remain truly biblical we must resist the temptation to narrow down the meaning or application of the kingdom of God to fit the particular bees in our bonnets. Each of us has our own particular bias, but we must not twist the scriptures to fit our interests.

All of us need the full-orbed teaching on the kingdom of God to correct our narrow vision and imbalance, to give us aspects of God's life-giving grace which we might otherwise lack.

2

IT'S GOD'S KINGDOM

Earthly kingdoms have clearly defined borders and can be marked out on a map. It is also clear which people belong as citizens. The kingdom of God is not like that. It does not have a geographical location and no particular group of people can claim it as theirs. God's sovereign rule stands above all humanly defined limitations. God's ways are higher than ours and his working breaks out of the neat boxes into which we try to fit him.

Those of us who travel widely see something of this. God's Spirit is moving in significant ways in many different denominations around the world. In many parts of Latin America the big development of the church is through the Pentecostals, although Baptists and others play their smaller role. In West Africa it is often through churches founded by interdenominational missions that the Holy Spirit works most freely. In East Africa we see the Lord mightily at work through the Anglican church. In Indonesia and Korea God's kingdom is extended most of all through traditional reformed Presbyterian churches. In South Africa and Singapore charismatic churches have brought new life to many.

The kingdom of God is not bound by our narrow ideas of how the Holy Spirit should function. We may like to dictate to God how he should work, but the Bible stresses that it is *God's* kingdom, not ours. 'The Lord reigns' (Ps. 93:1) – not us!

Political powers

Nor do political powers or even Satan himself hold the trump card. The Old Testament constantly reiterates the fact that the Lord alone is king; there is no other king. He will not tolerate rivals to his kingship, for he is a jealous God whose glory shall not be taken by another. And Paul assures us in 1 Corinthians 15:24 that ultimately every rival 'rule and every authority and power' will be destroyed.

One of the great titles of God is that he is King of kings. He is Lord over all human kingdoms and rulers. In Daniel 2 the prophet presents the great king Nebuchadnezzar with his dream and its interpretation, showing how God has given Nebuchadnezzar all the power, might and glory he enjoyed. It is by the will of the great King of kings that Nebuchadnezzar has become a lesser king of kings, to whom 'the God of heaven has given the kingdom' (Dan. 2:37). Then Daniel shows the king how his empire will be followed by a succession of lesser empires until the advent of the messianic kingdom 'which shall never be destroyed' (2:44). The King of kings rules over history and determines the course of earthly kingdoms. The book of Revelation also gives a prophetic sweep of history, showing that finally the Lamb will conquer the kings of this world, because the Lamb is 'Lord of lords and King of kings' (Rev. 17:14).

Even today it is easy for us to forget that political powers do not have supreme control. The great nations and their leaders strut across the stage of history as if there were no God over them. But the truth remains that the kingdom of God rules sovereignly over the kingdoms of this world.

The devil

The great usurper of God's kingly rule is Satan himself. Although in truth he is still under God's kingly rule, he has snatched for himself quite considerable power as the 'ruler of this world' (Jn. 12:31; 14:30; 16:11; Eph. 2:2). Sadly he is indeed ruler over this world and over the multitudes of people who do not acknowledge Jesus Christ as their lord and king. God, however, does not allow even

Satan to usurp his position as supreme king. When Jesus began his ministry he was immediately locked in battle with Satanic forces. He cast out demonic spirits, demonstrating his power over them, and he sent his disciples out to preach, heal and cast out demons. They rejoiced that the demons were subject to them in his name. Jesus then replied, 'I have given you authority . . . over all the power of the enemy' and he declared, 'I saw Satan fall like lightning from heaven' (Lk. 10:17–20). The culminating victory over the kingdom of the devil came through the death and resurrection of the incarnate Jesus. The prince of this world has been put down by the King of kings. The defeat of Satan will be finally completed in the great judgement. Meanwhile we rejoice that God is king over all demonic forces. We can defeat Satan now through the death of Jesus, by the word of our testimony and by our willingness to lay down our lives for the Lord (Rev. 12:11).

Miracles

The significance of the miracles Jesus performed – when he stilled the storm, healed the sick, cast out demons and raised the dead – was to demonstrate that 'the kingdom of God is at hand'. God's authoritative rule has come. His power has erupted into our midst. As

Jesus says, 'if it is by the Spirit of God that I cast out demons, then the kingdom of God has come upon you' (Matt. 12:28). When he sends his twelve disciples out to preach that the kingdom of heaven is at hand, he also commands them to heal, raise the dead and cast out demons. Once too in the book of Acts the preaching of the kingdom is linked to signs and great miracles being performed (Acts 8:12–13).

When the powerful kingdom of God is present, we may expect things to happen! We shall not be surprised that miracles take place. They are given in order to show that the Lord is king indeed and that no other power can rival him. But Jesus also warns us not to overemphasise signs and wonders, for we may easily be misled. False prophets may also show great signs and wonders, so that even God's chosen followers may perhaps be led astray (Matt. 24:24). All religions have their miracle-workers. Healings and apparent exorcisms are the normal stock-in-trade of special men or women in Islam, Hinduism, Buddhism, Judaism and all other faiths. Our God is characterised by humility, so he does not go in for sensationalism. Jesus even says that 'the kingdom of God is not coming with signs to be observed' (Lk. 17:20), but it is seen in the inner working of God which transforms our lives.

Christians in the West today are so insecure

about the very existence of God that we reach out hungrily for evidence of his powerful working. We devour stories of sensational miracles overseas and sadly there are some Christians who delight to write what we long to read.

Recently I read a report from Malaysia in a Christian magazine. I have worked in this country and have many friends there, so I was interested in what it had to say. My suspicions were raised by the very tone of the article. Truth was twisted to prove certain prejudices – the writer definitely had one or two axes to grind! And it was sensationalist. I therefore gave the article to several Christian leaders from Malaysia to ask them their opinion. All were agreed that the so-called miracles were largely fabricated and untrue. Even basic facts were unreliable.

It is true that our God demonstrates the reality of his unique kingdom by defeating Satan the usurper. Gracious miracles of power are an integral part of his kingdom. We may expect exorcism and other evidences that he alone is king. But let us not be gullible, swallowing every exciting story! Let us use the spiritual gift of discernment!

Church leaders

Political powers and Satan himself are not the only ones who may take God's glory to themselves. Church leaders too may be tempted to become authority figures. The biblical picture of leaders is that they are to be shepherds who should care for their sheep, give an example and lead the way. Shepherds are not authority figures. Ministers too are called to serve – that is the very meaning of the word 'minister' – not to rule over their people. Jesus makes this very clear in Mark 10:42–45. In the political world of the Gentiles, he says, their leaders 'exercise authority', but he then firmly rejects that for his followers – 'it shall not be so among you'. Like slaves Christian leaders should serve in humility. Like Jesus himself they are to give their lives for others, not try to rule with authority.

It is so easy to allow church leaders to take over the place of God in our lives. As Christians we are all a 'royal priesthood' (1 Pet. 2:9), all in God's kingdom and all priests with direct access to God himself. Of course we have much to learn from our leaders as more experienced, mature and gifted believers, but they are not the necessary mediators of God's word to us.

The outworking of God's kingdom

'Thy kingdom come', we ask in the Lord's Prayer (Matt. 6:9–13). We long that God's rule should be evident here on earth. We want him to be king in fact, not just in theory. But what does it mean for God to be king? The context of the Lord's Prayer gives us the answer.

'Hallowed be thy name . . .'

The coming of God's kingdom is linked inseparably to the honour of his name. In the Old Testament the purpose of Israel's national life was that the name of their God should be glorified both by Israel herself and also by the surrounding Gentile nations. In the New Testament too this is the goal of the church. We are to worship the Lord. Our lives should reflect his character so that other people will see God's holiness and glorify him. We live to bring him honour. We long that people of all nations everywhere might recognise his perfection and give him the honour that is his due.

In his diaries Christopher Columbus delights in his name 'Christopher'. It derives from the Latin and means someone who bears Christ. Columbus felt that in his journeys to the Americas he was taking Christ to the unevangelised peoples there. Whatever we may feel about his practice, his ideals were in this respect right.

Missionaries in remote tribal areas often talk of village children coming out to welcome the visiting missionary with cries of 'Jesus is coming; Jesus is coming.' We smile at the naiveté which thinks that the missionary is Jesus himself. But actually the children are right. As Christians we carry Christ within us. When we come, Christ comes. What a responsibility! Through us the name of the Lord is to be hallowed. When people see us, how much do they observe of the love, holiness, humility and perfection of our king?

I would not like it if people made rude remarks about my wife or children whom I love. I delight to hear appreciative comments about them. Likewise we hate to see the name of the Lord dragged in the mud and long for it to be properly honoured.

'Thy will be done . . .'

The coming of God's kingdom involves us in obedience to his will. Jesus said, 'If you love me, you will keep my commandments' (Jn. 14:15). What is the will of God? The answer is clear: 'this is the will of God, your sanctification' (1 Thess. 4:3). Paul goes on to say that 'whoever disregards this, disregards not man but God, who gives his Holy Spirit to you' (1 Thess. 4:8). God's will is that we should be holy, and that is why he has given us his Spirit. The very name of the Spirit is highly significant – he is the *Holy* Spirit. God enjoys our praise and worship; he rejoices when we open our mouths to share the gospel in witness to our friends; he encourages us to have faith that he will work all sorts of miracles; he loves to open his ears to our prayers. But all those things pale into insignificance when compared with God's great desire for us that we should be holy, righteous and pure.

This then is the primary will of God. But how can we discover the details of God's commandments to us? It is no use talking about obedience unless we know what he asks us to do.[1] God may speak to us in many ways, but the key is found in the study of his word, the Bible. As we soak ourselves in the scriptures, we shall grow in our understanding of the mind of Christ. We shall know him better and so also sense increasingly what he likes and what he does not like. God's revelation of himself has been preserved for us in the Bible so that we may know his will.

So when we talk about the kingdom, let us bear in mind its context of 'hallowed be thy name' and 'thy will be done'. The kingdom is for the honour of God rather than for the prosperity of man.

'The kingdom of our Lord and of his Christ' (Rev. 11:15)

The first three gospels give considerable emphasis to the kingdom, but in the epistles this changes. The kingdom is still mentioned

1 For a fuller treatment of how we can know God's will, see my *Finding Your Way* (IVP/STL, 1987).

from time to time, but now the writers are more interested in the central figure of the kingdom, Jesus himself, who is the Lord. Then in the final book of the New Testament, the book of Revelation, we are faced with the strange mixed metaphor of the royal lion of Judah who is the sacrificial Lamb of God (Rev. 5:5–6). And it is that Lamb who with God sits upon a throne (Rev. 22:1, 3). What a strange picture! The king is no longer the proud lion, but the meek Lamb which has been slaughtered in sacrifice.

What do we learn from all of this?

Jesus the Lord is central

On the first day of a holiday houseparty in Switzerland we all took the boat along the beautiful lake. The water reflected the clear blue sky and the splendid mountains. It seemed almost out of place to get into deep conversation, but soon we all began to get to know each other. The man next to me was an elder in a traditional evangelical church.

'Is your church growing?' I asked. 'Are you getting new people joining the congregation and coming to know the Lord?'

'No,' he replied. 'People don't seem to want the gospel these days. But we have a fine minister who really preaches the word.'

After some further talk I formed the impression that my friend came from a church which had made its doctrine into an idol and therefore could not find the life and love of Jesus Christ.

In the kingdom of God Jesus Christ is central. Nothing else must take his place, however good and important it may be. Even sound biblical doctrine can become the pride and emphasis of the church, rather than Jesus himself. Of course we need a right biblical understanding of the Lord and his work for us, but the key to the kingdom rests in a living relationship with Jesus Christ.

We all find it easy to slip into error. We put excellent but lesser things at the centre of the stage. There are various idols which may take the pre-eminent place from Christ in our churches – sound doctrine, the gifts of the Spirit, our form of worship or music, church tradition, miracles of healing, loving fellowship, good biblical scholarship. All of these are good and some even vital, but none of them serves any useful purpose if Jesus is toppled from his supreme throne. *He* is the king of the kingdom.

Just before this Swiss houseparty I had been studying 1 Corinthians as I lay in a hospital bed. The centrality of Jesus had impressed me. Wisdom and power are excellent, Paul declares. God himself is both wise and powerfully strong. But power and wisdom are found supremely in Jesus Christ (1 Cor. 1:24), so let us not get stuck on lesser things. Let us boast only in the Lord himself (1 Cor. 1:31).

Then I began a study of Colossians and was excited to notice the same point. Again Paul underlines that 'all things were created through *him* and for *him*' (Col. 1:16) so that *Christ* might be pre-eminent in all things (Col. 1:18).

Suffering and the kingdom

The book of Revelation spoke to a persecuted church with the triumphant message that the forces of evil will be vanquished and that God will triumph. The writer picked up the expression 'Lamb of God' from John 1:29 and from the whole sacrificial system of the Old Testament. He showed that, like the persecuted church, Jesus too suffered in apparently weak meekness as the Lamb who is sacrificed. It is that same meek Lamb who is worshipped with God as the King of kings. The kingdom belongs not only to God but also to his Messiah (Rev. 11:15) and the righteous will be vindicated.

The Bible contains this amazing paradox. God comes to earth in the form of a servant. He lays aside his glory. He is born not in a palace, but in a stable. He is rejected, despised and finally crucified. He is taken down from the cross, a cold corpse laid to rest in a dank tomb. We know that in theory he has the power not only to lay down his life but also to take it up again. But he has purposely shed his power. The New Testament therefore carefully uses a passive tense for the resurrection – Jesus *was raised*; he did not raise himself. He was dead, but God raised him up (Acts 2:32).

The foremost title for Jesus in the minds of the early apostles was 'the suffering servant'. The king does not just reign in glorious power; he suffers and serves like a slave.

As Christians we must learn an unnatural lesson. If we want to reign with Christ and enjoy the resurrection life of his kingdom, then we must follow in his footsteps of suffering and humble slave-like service. The slave enjoys no rights. So it is written that if we suffer and endure, then we shall also reign with Christ (2 Tim. 2:12). Paul knew the reality of fellowship with Christ in suffering. He therefore understood the true purpose of divine power in the Christian life. He did not want to use power to escape from sickness and suffering, but rather to enable us to persevere in endurance and joyful patience in the midst of suffering (Col. 1:11).

'May you be strengthened with all power, according to his glorious might,' Paul wrote. I can imagine some modern Christians reading that verse from Colossians and stopping at that point. Yes, power is the name of the game today. We want our mighty God to demonstrate his superiority and his reality by miraculous deeds of power. And he does! In his grace he loves to show weak Christians that he really does exist and that he does work today. He is also a jealous God who hates occult spirits or other deities being thought to be more glorious than he is. So he shows by signs and wonders that he is above them all. But Paul is not talking about that sort of thing in this verse. We must allow him to finish his sentence: 'May you be strengthened with all power, according to his glorious might, *for all endurance and patience with joy* . . .' And what a miracle that is! In Christ we can be given the glorious power to suffer with patient, joyful endurance.

The throne of God is occupied by a suffering Lamb. Sacrifice is the door to the kingdom. When Jesus saw that John the Baptist was in prison facing martyrdom, then he began to preach that the kingdom was at hand (Matt. 4:12, 17). Twenty-eight times the book of Revelation calls Jesus 'the Lamb' to underline this vital truth that entry into and enjoyment of God's kingdom means suffering service.

Some who advocate political revolution in order to establish the kingdom of God may find the biblical Jesus too weak for their liking. Others who believe that kingdom life means success-orientated prosperity may actually reject the suffering servant lamb as too poor. Yet others who emphasise God's miracles of healing leave little room for the reality of suffering and death. But the Bible clearly shows our Lord as weak and poor and one who suffered deeply. 'A servant is not greater than his master' (Jn. 13:16). As members of God's kingdom we too must be prepared to follow this difficult path.

3

ENTERING THE KINGDOM

In the last chapter we saw that the kingdom belongs to God. Happily our God loves to give with generous grace, so he shares the kingdom with us. As Jesus said, 'it is your Father's good pleasure to give you the kingdom' (Lk. 12:32).

How do we enter the kingdom?

It is when the kingdom is preached that we can understand it, appreciate it and enter into it. As Paul points out, we cannot believe without hearing, and we cannot hear without the preached word (Rom. 10:14).

But words have lost their credibility today. Many of us prefer political action or visible signs of the working of God's Spirit rather than 'mere preaching'. Of course the word should be accompanied by the visible signs of God at work, not only in the miraculous but also in the holiness and fellowship of God's people. But the Bible constantly stresses the central importance of words. It was by his word that God created the world and it was as the Word of God that Jesus came to serve us (Jn. 1). So we are not surprised to find that the New Testament talks much of the word or good news of the kingdom.

Repentance

When the reality of the kingdom comes near us, the first response should be repentance. We have already noted this emphasis in the preaching of the kingdom by John the Baptist and by Jesus himself. When we repent and God restores us to himself, he and all in heaven rejoice (Lk. 15:6, 10, 32).

What then is repentance? The Greek word signifies a complete about-turn of the mind, like a squad of soldiers turning round to march in the opposite direction. It should be noted firstly that it is the *mind* which changes direction, not just our actions. There is a constant emphasis in the Bible that our minds and our thinking direct the course of our lives.

Before we heard the message of the kingdom of God and his salvation we were under the control of Satan, whether we knew this consciously or not. He was the prince of our lives and he led us into sin and unbelief. Now we are to turn around and follow Jesus Christ as our supreme Lord and our guide. We shall come to hate the sin that spoilt our lives and stopped us giving God the honour due to him. Turning from Satan and sin, we now lovingly follow the Lord and obey him in holiness.

This repentance may well involve us in making restitution for the sin of the past. We may well have to confess to other people if we have in some way harmed them. We shall certainly have to confess our sin and say 'sorry' to God himself.

In entering the kingdom of God we are making a clean break with sin and the rule of Satan. If we have had occult connections in the past through Ouija boards, spiritism, witchcraft, Eastern religious practices, astrology or anything else which may open the door to evil spirits, then we need to repent of this and definitely break any link with it. We may well need prayerful help from others in order to clean out the demonic influence of Satan.

Faith

Together with repentance comes the need for faith. Faith is not just an academic exercise in which we are mentally assured that the good news of Jesus is the truth. Faith implies a definite trust in Christ as our Lord and Saviour. To trust someone is much more significant than just believing in their existence! I believe in the existence of the devil, but I don't trust him!

Believing in Christ is like getting into a swimming pool. There are lots of other people already in the water enjoying a good swim. How do you enter the water and join them? Some people dive in without hesitation, find the cold a shock but quickly adjust and enjoy it. Others go quietly to the shallow end, gently but unhesitatingly going deeper and deeper into the water until they launch themselves into a good swim. I tend to hover near the edge, feel the water with my toes and put off the climactic decision to dive into the cold water. Everybody assures me that it is lovely in, but my toes tell me that others' assessment may not be quite true! Finally, however, I know that a decision has to be taken, and I jump in. Sadly there are also some people who reject the advice of those who are already in the water and they determine not to swim at all. They miss so much.

Belief in Christ involves a commitment to him which is irrevocable. Some people come to this commitment quickly, some slowly. Some enter the kingdom gradually, step by step, while others dive in suddenly and decisively. How we enter does not matter. The fact that we do enter is what is important.

The cross and the resurrection

Some while back I was interviewing a young applicant to All Nations. He told me warmly of his conversion experience and enthused about his new faith. He was obviously enjoying his new experience of fellowship and worship with others of like mind. But as he talked I became increasingly uneasy.

What was the basis of his conversion? Who or what did he believe in? Faith is good, but to enter the kingdom of God it needs to be faith in Jesus Christ, his atoning death and resurrection. I asked him in what way the death of Jesus had been important for his conversion. Surprisingly he did not feel it had been important at all. After considerable further questioning I ended up with the impression that his faith and conversion were just a heart-warming emotional experience.

To enter the kingdom we require faith in the historical person of Jesus the Messiah. It is through his sacrificial death on the cross that we can be born again. On the cross he has taken the penalty of all our sin, opening the door for total forgiveness and cleansing.

A few months ago I was speaking at a Christian conference in Germany. At one stage I talked about the cross of Christ and the total cleansing we can obtain through his shed blood. A very respectable German businessman aged about sixty came to me at the end of the conference in tears. He had been involved in herding thousands of Jews into the gas chambers. Can the Christian's conscience ever be purified from such horrific sin? 'Yes,' I assured him. 'If we confess our sins, the blood of Jesus . . . cleanses from *all* sin' (1 Jn. 1:9, 7).

Perhaps our memories are not darkened by

such appalling evil, but many of us too find that certain misdemeanours in the past haunt us and we still feel unclean. It is good to be reminded that Christ's sacrificial death washes us totally.

Just as we are joined together with Christ in his death, so too we are raised with him to new life. God raised the cold corpse of Jesus from the grave – he lifts us up too from our past lives into the new resurrection life with Jesus Christ.

New birth

'Unless one is born anew, he cannot see the kingdom of God,' Jesus said to the godly Jewish leader Nicodemus (Jn. 3:3). We have to be transferred from the old life under Satan and sin before we can enter God's kingdom. Then we are raised to that new life in the resurrection. When we come to faith in Jesus Christ, we start a new spiritual life like a new-born baby starting its physical life.

We commonly translate John 3:3 as being 'born again', but actually the word used could mean 'born from above'. This experience is not only the start of a new life, it is also a birth which comes from above, from God himself. We cannot convert ourselves. This is the work of God in us and for us. We need the Lord to bring us into that new life where we can see God's kingdom and consciously come under his dominion.

Baptism and the Holy Spirit

The new birth is commonly linked to baptism and the gift of the Holy Spirit. In John 3 Jesus goes on to say that we cannot enter God's kingdom unless we are 'born of water and the Spirit' (Jn. 3:5). Water may here refer to baptism, but it could also be a delicate way of saying that we should not only be born as a result of sexual intercourse but also by the Spirit.

Baptism is the outward mark of belonging to God's people in the community of God's kingdom. It is the sign of the salvation God has promised to give all who believe in Jesus Christ. Repentance, faith, new birth and baptism go hand in hand. Then we need to add to that list the gift of the Holy Spirit. When we are born again, Jesus comes to live in us by his Spirit. Being born again includes receiving the Holy Spirit. Then as we grow in our new life we need to be constantly filled with the Spirit, so that he can make us increasingly like Christ in holiness, giving us all the fruit of the Spirit. He will also give to us those spiritual gifts which will be of benefit to the church and to ourselves. He will equip us for whatever ministries he calls us to.

How then do we enter the kingdom? By repentance and faith in the cross and resurrection of Jesus, by new birth from above, baptism and the Holy Spirit. So God redeems us and gives us eternal life through the forgiveness of our sin.

Conditions of entry

The outsider

Who can enter the kingdom? 'The pious, not ordinary people of the land – men, not women – Jews, not Gentiles.' This was the thinking of some at the time of Jesus. Jesus shatters such élitism by revealing himself more clearly to the woman of Samaria (Jn. 4:1–42) than to anyone else throughout his ministry on earth. She was certainly no model of pious decorum! And John 4 underlines the word 'woman' again and again to emphasise that Jesus was breaking through the male chauvinism of current religion. Even his disciples 'marvelled that he was talking with a woman' (Jn. 4:27)! And she was a Samaritan, not a Jew – 'Jews have no dealings with Samaritans' (Jn. 4:9).

As Donald Kraybill points out in his book *The Upside-Down Kingdom*, it is the poor, the outcast, the despised who are welcomed into the kingdom. The king invites to his feast the tramps who sleep by the roadside. The despised sinners and tax-collectors become his disciples. The rejects of respectable society are welcomed. Indeed it is shown to be much more difficult for the rich, the respectable and the powerful to enter the kingdom (Mk. 10:17–27).

The Pentecostal churches of Latin America illustrate this truth. Why do they grow so rapidly among the poor in the shanty towns? It is partly because these so-called dregs of society are thrilled to find that God esteems them. Being so poor, they cannot afford doctors, so services of healing attract them. The despised shanty-town person feels he is somebody in the church. Everyone calls him 'brother' or 'sister'; his testimony is greeted with cries of 'glory to God'. He can participate in the worship and be listened to with respect. And as he grows in Christian experience, he is given responsibility in church ministries. In the church and in the kingdom we all become people of significance. As Kraybill beautifully points out, in the kingdom 'everyone is the greatest'. Francis Schaeffer has said likewise that there are no 'little people' in the kingdom; all have the same status as God's children and heirs. The kingdom knows no hierarchy.

Humility

As we have seen, in Mark 10:17–27 Jesus teaches with shattering clarity how hard it is for the rich to enter the kingdom of God. Immediately before, people had brought children to Jesus (Mk. 10:13–16). He was in the middle of teaching his disciples and the children disturbed the peace. 'Don't bring the children in here! Get them out!' the disciples snapped. But Jesus was angry and said, 'Let the children come to me . . . for to such belongs the kingdom of God' (Mk. 10:14). If they belong to the kingdom, they can come to the king. To enter the kingdom we must become like little children – powerless and small. The Lord declares, 'this is the man to whom I will look, he that is humble and contrite in spirit, and trembles at my word' (Isa. 66:2). Was this word in Jesus' mind when he taught: 'Blessed are the poor in spirit, for theirs is the kingdom of heaven' (Matt. 5:3)?

Some years ago I did a Bible study on meekness and humility. I was challenged when this revealed that virtually all God's blessings and gifts are at some stage in scripture associated with meekness. Adult pride must give way to childlike meekness if we are to enter the kingdom. Vanity and self-assertiveness have no place under God's rule.

The cost

The Christian claims: 'Jesus is our king. We will do anything for him. We will go anywhere he wants us to serve him.'

The gospels call such self-sacrificing discipleship for the sake of Christ 'taking up our cross'. We are to nail our own desires and ambitions to the cross of Jesus so that we can then follow him in total slave-like obedience. Jewish rabbis called this total submission 'the yoke of the kingdom', so Jesus will have associated kingdom life with absolute obedience to God's law. He himself gave us the perfect example of this. In the Garden of Gethsemane he won through to the position where he could say to his heavenly Father 'not my will, but thine, be done' (Lk. 22:42). Happily we can rest assured that God's will is not that of an evil tyrant, but is 'good and acceptable and perfect' (Rom. 12:2). Such death to our own desires and natural selves leads to the new life of the resurrection in Christ. When we die in that way, the Holy Spirit of Christ can fill us and renew us. And that is far better than anything the world can offer!

'So therefore, whoever . . . does not renounce all that he has cannot be my disciple' (Lk. 14:33). Discipleship in the kingdom is radical. We need to count the cost before we enter God's kingdom and submit to his kingship. We shall be following a Lord who suffered. 'Foxes have holes, and birds of the air have nests; but the Son of man has nowhere to lay his head' (Lk. 9:58). Jesus goes on then to say, 'No one who puts his hand to the plough and looks back is fit for the kingdom of God' (Lk. 9:62). To such obedient believers he offers the new life of the kingdom, a joyful relationship with God the Father through Jesus Christ, and the fruit and ministry of the Spirit. This is the gift of eternal life.

Pass it on!

'Fellow workers for the kingdom of God' (Col. 4:11) – that is what God is looking for. Disciples of Christ are not only to enjoy the life of the kingdom for themselves, but also to work together with other believers in promoting God's kingdom in the world.

This is not a fun game; it will be hard work which will surely require disciplined obedience to Christ's word. Our work is '*for* the kingdom of God' and should lead to God's dominion being extended, so that new subjects are constantly being added to his kingdom. Such 'evangelism' or 'witness' longs for God's honour in the world and therefore that his rule should be acknowledged. Of course we also desire that other people should gain the salvation and rich blessings of the kingdom, but that is not our primary motive. We are called to be fellow-workers *for the kingdom of God*, that God may be king over all.

4
KINGDOM LIFE

A few years ago I was due to speak at a university Christian Union. I felt happy with the biblical exposition they had asked me to give as the message for that evening. Travel directions and questions of hospitality were all in order. But what about my appearance? The old days when speakers wore neat dark suits were definitely gone. Casual informal gear seemed the thing. At that stage men students were into shoulder-length hair, but I was too old for that. A compromise seemed in order – not too short, but not right down to the shoulders.

The meeting went well and the students were enthusiastic. The Lord had spoken and brought blessing.

The next day I drove to a more traditional church for the weekend. I duly put on my dark blue suit and respectable tie. But what about my hair? My wife reminded me that Sunday lunch would be taken with two elderly prayer supporters. A conservative hair-style was required. My wife gave me a trim and I set off in the car.

'It's good to see you don't have long straggly hair like so many men these days,' one of the ladies greeted me. I shared with her the difficulty of being all things to all men unless one possessed a range of wigs for all styles of meeting. I assured her that to me the length of one's hair has no significance whatsoever. It is sad that little details of that nature can open or close peoples' ears to the word of God. I was reminded of Paul's word in Romans 14:17, 'the kingdom of God is not food and drink [nor hair-style or clothing] but righteousness and peace and joy in the Holy Spirit'.

The life of the kingdom has immeasurably rich characteristics. It seems a pity to give too much importance to trivial legalistic details. Paul himself was free to place himself under the restrictions of the law if that would help him win for Jesus Christ those who were under the law (1 Cor. 9:19–23). But he was also happy to be free from the law for those who boasted of their freedom. How free are we? Are we happy to be old-fashioned and legalistic when that is appropriate, but also free and informal when that fits?

Above all, we should be positive! The kingdom, Paul says, is righteousness, peace and joy in the Holy Spirit (Rom. 14:17).

Righteousness

'When Messiah comes, he will bring in a kingdom of righteousness. When Israel is righteous even just for a moment, then the kingdom will come.' So the Jewish people have asserted for centuries, linking the coming of the kingdom of heaven with holy righteousness. And still today Jews question the Christian claim that the kingdom has come through the person of Jesus, because they note that holy righteousness has not yet been established.

Wonderfully the New Testament stresses that the coming of God's kingdom does not have to be earned by our righteousness, but is a gift of God's abounding and merciful grace. Although we are sinners and do not reach God's perfect standards of righteousness, yet Jesus takes our sin on to his own shoulders, bears that sin for us on the cross and then gives us his righteousness. Talking of Jesus Christ, Paul says that God 'made him to be sin who knew no sin, so that in him we might become the righteousness of God' (2 Cor. 5:21). So God covers us and our sin with the cloak of his own perfect righteousness. When God therefore looks at us, all he sees is Christ and his righteousness. Paul loves to say that we are 'in Christ' (e.g. Rom. 8:1). 'Blessed are those . . . whose sins are covered' (Ps. 32:1 quoted in Rom. 4:7). In Christ we are reckoned to be righteous despite our sin.

The traditional Jewish emphasis on kingdom righteousness is particularly clear in the apostle Paul's writings. While clearly teaching that we as sinners are reckoned to be righteous in God's eyes, Paul nevertheless stresses the absolute necessity of actual righteousness in daily living. The majority of his references to the kingdom relate to the question of holiness in everyday behaviour. He repeatedly warns that unholy people will not inherit or enter into God's kingdom and so he urges his readers to lead lives that are worthy of God (1 Cor. 6:9–10; Gal. 5:19–21; Eph. 5:5; 1 Thess. 2:10–12; 2 Thess. 1:5). The writer to the Hebrews likewise quotes from Psalm 45:6–7 to affirm, 'the righteous sceptre is the sceptre of thy kingdom. Thou hast loved righteousness and hated lawlessness' (Heb. 1:8–9). Matthew, the great writer on the kingdom, also underlines this connection between the kingdom and righteousness. The kingdom sermon, called the Sermon on the Mount, emphasises righteousness and exhorts us all to 'seek first his kingdom and his righteousness' (Matt. 6:33).

The Jews have traditionally taught that the kingdom will come only when Israel demonstrates true righteousness. While the New Testament continues that emphasis on righteousness, it is aware that actually all of us fail and sin sneaks into all our lives all the time. Therefore the coming of God's kingdom through Jesus Christ rebukes us for our sin and calls us to repentance. If we are to be people of the kingdom here on earth we must be marked by holiness of living. And if we are to inherit the fullness of the kingdom in the glory of eternal life, then we must demonstrate righteousness. This is the work of the Holy Spirit in us. He it is who can change us into the very likeness of Christ and transform us into holy people.

Justice

An oppressive regime suppressed the demands of the people. The occupying army served the interests of the foreign imperialist power. Human rights were trampled into the dust. Religious sensitivities were flouted. The Jewish people in this context remembered all the prophetic promises of a national deliverer. Messianic expectations ran high. Various charismatic figures had gathered crowds around them and begun rebellions against the Romans, only to be mercilessly crushed. Was Jesus of Nazareth the true Messiah? Would he be the new king like David of old who had led Israel into its heyday of national prosperity and power? Would Jesus be the king to defeat the Romans and deliver Israel? Rumours of a political messianic king ran through the Jewish crowds like wildfire.

What a disappointment! Jesus firmly denied that he was that sort of king. He didn't go in for violent revolution. His disciples and he remained unarmed. When the crowds wanted to make him their king, he slipped away from them to avoid such prominence. He even said, 'My kingship is not of this world; if my kingship were of this world, my servants would fight' (Jn. 18:36). And his triumphal entry into Jerusalem was not on a war-horse, but riding on a donkey. Jesus is the meek servant king, not the powerful political figure people hoped for.

But the life and message of Jesus does have socio-political significance. At the outset of his ministry he applied to himself the words of Isaiah 61 that he was to preach good news to the poor, release to captives, recovery of sight to the blind, liberty for the oppressed (Lk. 4:18–19). His message so disturbed the status quo that both religious and political authorities were threatened and crucified him as 'king of the Jews'. As Schechter points out,[1] 'bad government is incompatible with the kingdom of God'. Why is that?

In the Old Testament righteousness and justice are linked together like Siamese twins. They must not be separated. Justice *is* righteousness expressed in society. Personal and individual righteousness should go hand in

1 Schechter, *Aspects of Rabbinic Theology*, p. 106.

hand with a deep concern for social righteousness. Traditionally in Jewish thought on the kingdom of heaven, righteousness and justice together were to characterise the life of the kingdom. It is of course vitally important that each of us develops a true purity of life and we all know the scandal caused by financial, sexual or other forms of sin. But God is equally concerned about our social relationships in society, at work, in our community, at home. In fact Paul's injunction to be filled with the Spirit leads on to a long section about our social relationships (Eph. 5:18–6:9). And it is in the context of these social relationships that he gives his famous teaching about our need to put on the whole armour of God (Eph. 6:10–20). God hates it when his children engage in warm worship and lead morally upright lives, but oppress their employees at work or indulge in élitist attitudes to people of other racial backgrounds.

Feed the hungry, give water to the thirsty, clothe the naked, visit the sick and those in prison. So Jesus urged his followers. Then the king will say: 'Come, O blessed of my Father, inherit the kingdom prepared for you' (Matt. 25:34–36).

The Christian is called to help the needy and alleviate the sufferings of those who are poor and oppressed. It is deeply distressing to see the fearful injustices between the 'haves' and the 'have-nots', particularly in our cities and in developing countries around the world. God himself sides with such marginalised people. Jesus showed particular concern for despised publicans and sinners, children, women, Gentiles, harlots. Kraybill called his book *The Upside-Down Kingdom*: the kingdom of God is not for the rich and powerful so much as for the poor and despised.

But such social concern may sometimes prove inadequate. We may need to deal with the political causes of social sufferings. Let me give an example.

A missionary couple in Latin America felt a deep compassion for the girls who came into the big cities from their country background. The missionaries broke their hearts as they saw these simple girls being trapped by rich and powerful men who ensnared them in prostitution rackets. The missionaries began to befriend some of these girls, bringing them into the fellowship of the church and opening the door to a new life. Some of the girls began to leave the brothels, encouraged and helped by the Christian community. Then two men visited the missionaries. 'If you don't leave our girls alone, you will be in trouble,' they threatened. The men warned them that civic, military and police leaders were actually running these prostitution rackets. If the missionaries were roughed up, their children molested and their homes destroyed, it would be no use expecting justice from the authorities! What should they do?

Evangelistic witness and social concern soon got those missionaries into political issues up to their necks. This would have been equally true had they tried to help poor peasants suffering at the hands of greedy landlords and the grave inequalities of land ownership. It is no use Christians claiming to be apolitical. Justice may demand political involvement.

While in the Old Testament the twin words 'righteousness' and 'justice' occur together with great frequency, in the New Testament the idea of justice is clearly present but the word is missing. I would like to suggest that the word 'fellowship' takes its place. In the Old Testament justice was to be practised primarily in the community of God's people Israel; in the New Testament fellowship is also within God's people, the church.

What is fellowship? A cup of coffee together? Prayer and praise together? Well, it may include both of those, but fellowship is much deeper than that. The kingdom life means such richly loving community life that we are willing to share even our material possessions for the good of all. The early church so loved each other that they voluntarily shared their goods (Acts 2:44–45; 4:32) – the word used by Luke for 'in common' has the same root as the word for 'fellowship'.

Kingdom life breaks down all the barriers of colour, wealth and status. Love motivates us to remove any hindrance to such fellowship by the appropriate sharing of all we have and all we are. Justice is to be practised in loving fellowship in the Christian community. The kingdom life is not individualistic, but involves us in the community of God's people. And God's people are not just to enjoy selfishly the rich privilege of belonging to God in his kingdom, we are to serve the wider community in society. Righteousness and justice/fellowship will be seen primarily within God's church, but we are to work and preach to spread it in the world.

Peace

'Seal your love with a kiss,' the minister said to a young couple at a wedding I was attending. A kiss is the outward sign of union together. 'Righteousness and peace will kiss each other', the psalmist wrote (Ps. 85:10). Paul confirms this in Romans 5:1, where he affirms that we have peace with God because we are reckoned to be righteous through our faith in Jesus Christ. Isaiah too saw that in the messianic kingdom peace, righteousness and justice would go together – 'Of the increase of his government and of peace there will be no end, upon the throne of David and over his kingdom . . . with justice and with righteousness' (Isa. 9:7).

Peace with God
Thanks to the sacrificial death of Jesus on our behalf, God becomes our father and friend. The holy judge has become the loving Father. We have been reconciled with God and can now live in a relationship of peace with him.

Because of bad experiences with their earthly father many people find it hard to enjoy that peace which Jesus has won for us. They always feel that God is distant, uncaring or unduly demanding. As a result they may fear God and serve him without a right enjoyment of peace. If this is true of you, share it with another Christian and allow them to pray with you and love you. Take time to meditate on your heavenly Father's unchanging and unconditional grace and love.

Peace in the church
Two ladies in the church did not agree with each other and they quarrelled. A typical church scenario? It may be, but Paul was so worried about it that he wrote to the Philippian church and urged the two ladies to make it up (Phil. 4:2–3). He realised that it would help if others in the church encouraged and assisted them towards reconciliation. And he showed them all the basis for peaceful relationships – the humble self-sacrificing example of Jesus. We are to be like Jesus in

doing nothing out of selfishness or pride. Then we will find it easier to be loving and of one mind (Phil. 2:1–8).

'It is beautiful how Jewish and German Christians can be reconciled and can love one another as Christians,' I observed to a Jewish Christian who shared the platform with me in a meeting. He smiled ruefully. 'I wish I could win through to actually loving Germans. Many of my family perished in the gas chambers and I still cannot forgive the German people, even German Christians.' How well one understands, but failure to forgive will blight Christian growth.

The heart of the Christian message lies in God's forgiveness, reconciliation, peace and love. Our lives deny these fundamental truths if we do not live in loving peace with our brothers and sisters in Christ. But what joy it is to experience the living reality of Christian fellowship and community.

Peace with our neighbour

'So far as it depends on you, live peaceably with all' (Rom. 12:18). People may dislike, criticise or do bad things to us, but the Christian should not reciprocate and return evil for evil.

I was staying with someone recently whose next-door neighbour had had some bad experience of Christians as a young person. Now he was furious that his neighbours were Christian. He refused ever to greet them or speak to them. They tried every possible sign of friendliness, but he snubbed them. Then he began damaging their garden fence and knocking down their flowers. What should they do? In theory the answer was simple – be patient, go on loving, from their side having an attitude of peace towards him. I also joined them in prayer that their neighbour would either move house or come to a transforming faith in Jesus Christ – preferably the latter!

Peace within ourselves

Books on pastoral counselling abound today with their insightful teaching on the development of our personality. We need this. We live in a rat-race society with its fast-changing culture, unstable or broken marriages, no security of employment, depersonalised relationships at work and in society. This all leaves its mark on us. Many today feel such personal insecurity and lack of self-value that it is hard to enjoy the serenity of inner peace. Some may be helped by prayer ministry, others by pastoral counselling; all will need the supportive love of fellow Christians and encouragement to meditate on the abiding love and grace of Jesus Christ.

Joy in the Holy Spirit

The third characteristic of kingdom life listed by Paul in Romans 14:17 is joy in the Spirit.

Jesus told his disciples that they should particularly rejoice because their names were written in heaven (Lk. 10:20). The assurance of eternal life gives us even greater joy than seeing demons cast out or other miraculous signs of God in action, Jesus tells them.

In the kingdom we have the joy of being adopted as God's children and heirs. We not only rejoice to have God as our loving Father, but we also inherit all the riches of his grace. In the life of the kingdom he delights to fill us with his Spirit, who will graciously give us his fruit of holy living (Gal. 5:22–23) and those gifts which will enable us to play our part in the edification of his church.

It is sad when Christians are known as people with long faces. The New Testament constantly encourages us to be full of thanksgiving and rejoicing. As Christians we have so much for which to thank the Lord and so much to rejoice in. In Jesus' kingdom sermon, on the mountainside, the word for 'blessed' actually means 'happy'. 'Happy are the poor in spirit; happy are those who mourn; happy are the meek' (Matt. 5:3–11). This does not mean a glib, 'Smile, Jesus loves you,' which can be very forced and superficial. But the kingdom life imparts a deep-seated contentment and joy even in the midst of bereavement or other suffering. The Spirit makes us into people of joy.

This joy should also be shown in our

worship. Even in times of deep repentance and confession or in times of quiet meditation our worship should be characterised by that same deep contentment in Christ.

Praise and worship form an integral part of life in God's kingdom. As the old rabbis have said, 'If there be no peoples praising him, where is the glory of the king?' Some of the great psalms of worship are known as the kingdom psalms (e.g. Ps. 2; 18; 20; 45; 72). They were composed to express the joyful worship of God's people. From early times the Spirit has led God's people into worship through singing. Paul too talks of singing 'psalms and hymns and spiritual songs with thankfulness in your hearts to God' (Col. 3:16) – is it significant for us today that such praise is expressed in psalms, hymns and spiritual songs?! Let us be free to utilise a rich variety of musical forms in our worship. Paul also stresses here that our singing is 'with thankfulness' and it is 'to God', not just a good musical experience for our own satisfaction.

Power, not empty talk (1 Cor. 4:20)

The Jews had such reverence for the name of God that they hesitated to utter that sacred word, preferring to use some other synonym. One such was 'power' – so Jesus talked of himself sitting at 'the right hand of Power'

(Mk. 14:62). God was known as a God of dynamic power. He is not some cool deity sitting in the clouds impotently observing the world from on high. He is the God who by his word created the world and since then has been passionately concerned and active in the affairs of men. So it is not surprising that in the Lord's Prayer the kingdom, the power and the glory go together (Matt. 6:13, RSV footnote). Paul too knows that the kingdom comes in power, not in empty verbiage (1 Cor. 4:20) – the contrast is power versus empty words, not power versus words in general, for the context shows Paul using words to admonish and teach in the churches.

We expect our God to demonstrate his power. But how and to what effect?

At particular and significant times in history God has poured out evident signs of his power, but he has done so in markedly different ways. At the time of the exodus from Egypt God used Moses to show Pharaoh his miraculous power and to provide for the progress and daily needs of Israel. Then there was a remarkable outburst of miraculous signs in the time of Elijah and Elisha to underline the significance of their ministry in turning Israel away from the worship of Baal back to the true God. Both with Moses and with Elijah and Elisha God's power was shown through miracles.

The next climactic period of Israel's history

was the age of the great prophets. In the space of just a few decades most of the Old Testament prophets lived and fulfilled their ministry. This time, however, God's power was not shown in sensational miracles, but rather through the power of his word. Still today we marvel at God's powerful word when we read Isaiah, Jeremiah and the other great prophets of that era.

After the great prophets Israel went through several centuries when God seemed to have withdrawn behind the clouds. What excitement then when the powerful words of John the Baptist captivated the crowds! And then Jesus the Messiah himself! The king and the kingdom had come. Again power was seen in Jesus' authoritative teaching and in the miracles he worked. People were amazed at his teaching and bowled over by his miracles – healing the sick, raising the dead, stilling the storm, casting out demons, producing money in a fish's mouth.

The early church followed in Jesus' footsteps. By the Holy Spirit their teaching and preaching produced powerful results. Their words were accompanied by miraculous signs. The gospels carefully link word and sign together. John's gospel follows each miraculous sign with a chunk of Jesus' teaching. Matthew has long chapters filled with stories of Jesus' powerful works and then a long section of his teaching. Work and word must not be separated. In the Acts of the Apostles likewise the early Christians preach the gospel in power and demonstrate its reality by signs following.

Some Christians claim that after the first century miracles died out in the Christian church. This is historically untrue. It does seem to be true that in the Western church the emphasis was largely on preaching and teaching rather than on miracles of healing or exorcism. So God's power was demonstrated by great preaching. In the Eastern church, however, in Egypt and the Middle East, the desert fathers and monks continued to expect God's power to be shown through miracles of healing and exorcism as well as miracles of power over nature.

In the so-called Dark Ages a great struggle took place to win the pagan tribes of Europe to the faith of Jesus Christ. How did God's power manifest itself during this vital period of God's working in history? It was seen in the courageous, self-sacrificing faith of the intrepid Celtic missionaries. Although we might query some aspects of their doctrine, their deep spirituality and daring vision revealed the reality of God's sovereign reign.

Perhaps the next crucial period of church history was the Reformation. Again we do not see much evidence of sensational miracles, but we do see God's power at work, transforming not only individual lives but also the whole development of European religion and culture. God's power gave the Reformers an amazingly clear grasp of biblical essentials despite the prevailing religious corruption. When one reads Luther's or Calvin's commentaries, one is struck by their tremendous gift of biblical understanding and exegesis. These giant intellectual gifts were matched by self-sacrificing faith. Many of the Reformers died the death of a martyr. They were willing to pay the ultimate price to release God's power through the open Bible. And in fact God's word changed the whole course of European history – that is surely God's power in action! And the Bible still retains its ability by the Spirit to change lives.

In this past century particularly we have seen God powerfully at work in the growth of his church throughout the world. The modern missionary movement has again demonstrated God's universal power. Sometimes healings and exorcisms have been an integral part of the missionary outreach, sometimes powerful preaching and teaching have been God's tool, sometimes the self-sacrificing lives of humble, loving Christian workers have been the proof of God's grace and power.

In Britain today we are seeing much more miraculous working than in previous times. In my own life too God's miraculous working in answer to prayer has played a significant role. There are exciting reports of remarkable miracles in much of Latin America and in China. But for some reason this does not seem generally to be the case in the Soviet Union or Afghanistan, despite the fearful persecution and material deprivation of oppressed Christians.

Miracles have no importance in themselves. They are merely one possible evidence or sign of God's kingdom at work. God is supremely concerned for the faith and holiness of his church and people. If miracles will help us believe with true holiness, then he may well give us such signs. If other demonstrations of the power of the kingdom suit us better, he fits his working to our needs. He is a God of loving grace.

When God does graciously give us miracles of healing, we need to remember that the kingdom is not yet perfectly present. There is still a future dimension to the kingdom, as we shall see in our next chapter. We are not therefore surprised when sickness and death are not totally overcome in this world. God knows when we need sickness to help us grow in faith and holiness, patience and hope. In a fallen world sickness and death are still a necessary part of our experience in life, but God gives grace to endure. Through suffering we may grow in our own character, in our relationship with the Lord and in our ability to counsel and help others in need. Sometimes he graciously heals us and delivers us from suffering, but sometimes he allows our sufferings to continue. This is the mystery of God's sovereignty and it is unwise for us to try to force God into our patterns. He is no genie of the lamp who will respond automatically to our faith and give us all we want. The Japanese theologian Kosuke Koyama has warned us of the danger of trying to 'domesticate God', making him into a domestic animal who does our bidding whenever we pray. God is king, not us!

We walk a tightrope. We may so stress miracles of healing that we face problems of faith when Christians are not healed or die. This is unreal and overemphasises the fact that the kingdom has already come without taking due note of the fact that the kingdom is not yet here in its fullness. Others of us may underemphasise God's miracle-working power and by our lack of faith quench the Spirit.

We believe in an all-powerful God. He can do all things. And we are his instruments if his Spirit is in us. He will demonstrate his sovereign kingly rule as he wills, to bring glory and honour to his name.

Universality

Right at the outset of his teaching ministry Jesus took the bull by the horns – God's grace was not just for Jews, but also for Gentiles of all races. The great prophet Elijah was sent to a Gentile woman in Sidon rather than to an Israelite widow. Elisha was used to bring healing to the Syrian Naaman, not to any of the lepers in Israel (Lk. 4:24–27).

Jesus surely knew that the best of Jewish tradition understood that the messianic kingdom would be for *all* peoples – and there has been a major strand of rabbinic teaching ever since which has stressed the universality of the kingdom. In the final messianic banquet people from all nations will share the feast together (Matt. 8:11).

In Matthew 14 Jesus fed a great crowd of some five thousand Jewish men plus an undisclosed number of women and children. No one queried his doing this. Even the Jewish authorities did not object to him feeding Jewish crowds. But in the following chapter we read of him miraculously feeding a further crowd of four thousand men. This was in a Gentile area and the indications are that it must have been a Gentile crowd. Feeding Gentiles – was this a sign of the messianic banquet? What right did Jesus have to do this? The Jewish leaders demanded proof from heaven (Matt. 16:1). Jesus replied with the enigmatic words that they would receive only the 'sign of Jonah' (Matt. 16:4). What did this mean? Was Jesus referring to Jonah's three days and nights inside the great fish and thus to his own death, burial and resurrection? Or was he referring to the fact that Jonah was the only Old Testament prophet to be sent to preach to Gentiles in Nineveh?

The God of Israel is king in all the four corners of the world. The coming of his kingdom therefore requires that the gospel be preached to all nations – 'and then the end will come' (Matt. 24:14). In the fullness of the kingdom there must be people from every tribe, tongue, people and nation around God's heavenly throne to worship him (Rev. 5:9–14). We cannot experience the fullness of the kingdom life until we share in worship with people of all races, colours, ages and backgrounds.

This was the big issue in the New Testament church. Would the God of Israel accept Gentiles as followers of the Jewish Messiah without them joining the Jewish community and becoming like Jews? Is the Christian faith universal? Much of the New Testament deals with this question.[2] And it is still an issue today. Some Christians are so deeply involved in their own area of ministry that they have no interest in the rest of the world. Others even

2 For a fuller theological discussion of this, see J. Blauw's *The Missionary Nature of the Church* (Butterworth Press, 1962), R. de Riddler's *Discipling the Nations* (Baker Book House, 1971) and the New Testament section of D. Senior and C. Stuhlmueller's *Biblical Foundations for Mission* (S.C.M., 1983). For a more popular overview, see my *Don't Just Stand There* (IVP/STL, 1976).

wonder whether people of other races and religions need Jesus Christ and the gospel. 'Are not other religions equally valid?' they ask. 'Arabs are Muslim, Indians are Hindu, Japanese are Buddhist, Jews are Judaists and Europeans used to be Christians.' The New Testament denies such ideas and shows Jesus Christ as the king of all peoples everywhere.

God's mercies in his kingdom are for both Jews and Gentiles (Rom. 11:11–32). It is in this context of God's mercies that Paul appeals to his readers to present their bodies as living sacrifices (Rom. 12:1). He does not ask us to give our spirits in God's service, but our bodies – Paul is so practical and down-to-earth! It's our bodies he wants! And probably our spirits will follow wherever our bodies go!

This, Paul says, is true spiritual worship (Rom. 12:1). Worship in the Spirit means self-sacrificing service in order that the mercies of God might reach out to Jews and Gentiles of all nations.

It is unbiblical to be narrow and insular in our attitudes. If we do not have a world-wide vision, we do not have the mind of Christ and we are missing a fundamental element in kingdom life. As George Beasley-Murray says in his major work on the kingdom of God, the nature of the kingdom is universality, righteousness and peace. These three form the heart of biblical teaching on the life of the kingdom. They should remain central in all we say, sing or think today about kingdom life.

5

IT HAS COME, IT WILL COME

Preaching in a strongly evangelical German church I was painting the exciting picture of God's plan for the future. I concluded by encouraging the Christians to pray, work and witness with that glorious goal in mind. Using Habakkuk 2:14 we noted the fact that the whole earth 'will be filled with the knowledge of the glory of the Lord, as the waters cover the sea'. When God's kingdom is complete, his glory will not be restricted to a few people hidden away in obscure corners. The whole earth will see his splendour in fullness. Every street in every town all over the world will be filled with the majestic presence of the living God.

The verse in Habakkuk related to Paul's parallel picture of 'the full number of the Gentiles' coming into God's kingdom and 'all Israel' being saved (Rom. 11:25–26). How we all must look forward to this great climax of history – those huge crowds of people from every nation and people, including multitudes of the Jewish race!

One of the church elders came to me after the service and thanked me warmly for my message. 'We must wait patiently and pray,' he said, 'for of course that glorious future day will only come when Jesus returns. Meanwhile we must just endure the godlessness of this age.'

My heart sank. My message had failed. Yes, I had excited people with the vision of the future, but somehow they had failed to see that we are already called now to be God's fellow-workers (1 Cor. 3:9; 2 Cor. 6:1) in moving towards the goal of God's perfect kingdom. It is of course true that we shall never achieve the perfection of God's kingdom life in this world, for that will indeed only come when Jesus returns in glory at his second coming. But meanwhile it is our happy task to move forward towards the fullness of life in the kingdom. Our evangelisation will extend God's rule increasingly. And then when the good news of the kingdom has been preached throughout the whole world to all nations, 'the end will come' (Matt. 24:14).

It is not only by world-wide evangelisation that we work towards the fullness of the kingdom. The apostle Peter says we are not only to wait for the kingdom, but also to hasten its coming (2 Pet. 3:12). But how does he say we can do that? His answer is straightforward: by 'lives of holiness and godliness' (2 Pet. 3:11). The perfect kingdom life will be seen in absolute holiness of life, both individually and in our relationships together. In the glory there will be no more sin. We shall experience unclouded love, the best that God can give us, the most 'excellent way' (1 Cor. 12:31). All other gifts will pass away, but complete trust in the Lord, assured hope which no longer experiences doubt, and the bliss of full love will go on and on for ever – this is eternal life. Such love for God and for other believers leaves no room for sin. We shall serve the Lord and worship him in perfect holiness and in complete harmony with all those who together with us are gathered around the throne of God.

Such a life of perfection in the kingdom requires a little practice now! It is the work of God's Holy Spirit to prepare us for eternal life.

Although the full perfection of kingdom life remains in the future, Jesus declared that it has already begun. This is the paradox of the biblical teaching on the kingdom. When Jesus the king came to earth two thousand years ago, he ushered in the kingdom. In the person of Jesus the kingdom has erupted into the world. And yet we await its full perfection and therefore pray 'thy kingdom come' in the Lord's Prayer. The Beatitudes in Matthew 5:3–12 reflect this paradox by using both present and future tenses – 'Blessed *are* . . . for they *shall* . . .'

Our knowledge of the future affects the way we live now, our aims in life and what we expect God to be doing in our midst. The perfect future gives us confidence even in difficult times now.

While it is true that we shall reign with Christ in the heavenly kingdom, we must not allow competitive pride to spoil our lives and relationships. This problem afflicted the first disciples of Jesus, and in our own different way we can fall into the same temptation. James and John betrayed their wrong attitudes through two requests. First: 'We want you to do for us whatever we ask of you' (Mk. 10:35). This demand shows they were looking rather for their own glory than for the glory of the Lord. But kingdom life is not selfish. It does not ask about the benefits we may get out of faith in Christ, but longs for Jesus Christ to be honoured.

The second request was equally disastrous! 'Grant us to sit, one at your right hand and one at your left, in your glory' (Mk. 10:37). As faithful disciples they expected and asked for the best positions in the kingdom. Surely they were better Christians than other people, they thought, so doubtless Jesus would be glad to honour them in this way. How easily selfish pride convinces us that we are superior to other believers! But they had a totally wrong idea of what Jesus' 'glory' actually meant. They thought of him on his kingdom throne in the splendour of the messianic banquet – and they wanted to share with him in that joy. But Jesus' glory is actually experienced in the suffering of his crucifixion, which Jesus calls 'my hour'. When he is about to be crucified he says, 'Now is the Son of man glorified' (Jn. 13:31). Who then would sit at Jesus' right and left in his glory? Two thieves! James and John had quite a wrong idea of kingdom life! As we wait and prepare for the fullness of the kingdom, our way will include suffering.

But gloriously there is a resurrection beyond the cross and peace beyond all present suffering. In God's perfect kingdom the Lord will be perfectly with us and we with him (Rev. 21:3). The consequence of this unclouded relationship of God with us is that 'he will wipe away every tear . . . death shall be no more neither shall there be mourning nor crying nor pain any more'. Satan will be totally removed from the scene, sin will be no more, all will be blissfully perfect. What a prospect to warm our hearts!

Revelation 21 links our full salvation in the kingdom with the tragic judgement of those whose sin reflects the nature of Satan (Rev. 21:8) – the cowardly, faithless, polluted, murderers, fornicators, sorcerers, idolaters and liars. Together with the devil, the false prophet and all whose names are not in Christ's book of life (Rev. 20:10, 14) they will be judged and thrown into 'the lake of fire'.

We have been warned! It is not only God's wonderful love and grace which thrust us out into the world to bring people into Christ's sure salvation; it is also the fact that people need to be saved from such a fearful judgement.

And we too need to be ready for the coming of Jesus in glory and for the day of judgement. In chapter 1 we listed some of the 'kingdom parables', but we omitted one that is important in this context. 'The kingdom of heaven shall be compared to ten maidens' (Matt. 25:1). The story is well known (Matt. 25:1–12). Five of the young women kept their lamps trimmed and ready, so they could welcome the bridegroom when he came. The five foolish ones failed to take oil for their lamps in preparation – presumably they did not expect the bridegroom to come yet. Jesus' parable graphically declares that as a result 'the door was shut' and despite their desperate cries of 'Lord, lord' the bridegroom said 'I do not know you.'

The punch-line of the story is 'Watch therefore, for you know neither the day nor the hour' (Matt. 25:13). Jesus may come at any time, so be constantly ready. Ever since the days of Jesus on earth his followers have expected the imminent return of Christ. He actually said to his disciples 'there are some standing here who will not taste death before they see the kingdom of God' (Lk. 9:27).

There are various possible interpretations of this verse, but as a result of such sayings Jesus' followers expected him to return very soon. Each generation since then has also thought he would come back in their time. And we today must also be ready and eager for his return.

The climax

In chapter 2 we saw that 'It's God's kingdom'; and now again we must finish the book by underlining the whole purpose of the kingdom life. It is 'that God may be everything to every one' (1 Cor. 15:28). It is good to have talked about righteousness and holiness, justice, miraculous signs and other characteristics of our experience of God's reign. But these are just means to an end. The purpose of everything is that God himself may be king over all.

All three persons of the Trinity show wonderful self-effacing humility.

The Holy Spirit glorifies Jesus, not himself. As Jesus said when talking about the work of the Holy Spirit, 'he will take what is mine and declare it to you' (Jn. 16:14–15). Whenever the Holy Spirit is clearly at work, people talk very little about the Spirit, but rather glorify Jesus Christ and talk much about him.

Jesus comes to earth to reveal the Father

and to open the way for us to relate with the Father. Just as the Spirit points away from himself in order to glorify the Son, so now the Son's ministry is to be the way to the Father and to glorify him.

In his final great prayer before the crucifixion Jesus not only prays that the Father will glorify him (Jn. 17:1, 5), but also talks confidently of the glory that the Father has given to him (Jn. 17:22, 24). So the Spirit glorifies the Son, whose ministry it is to glorify the Father. The Father then delights in giving glory to his Son, for even God the Father is amazingly humble.

But the final act in the life of the kingdom is that the Son gives all the glory back to the Father (Jn. 17:1). When the end comes, Jesus 'delivers the kingdom to God the Father' and destroys all possible rivals to his supreme reign (1 Cor. 15:24). This destruction of all rivals to the kingdom of God began with the miracles of Jesus, when he cast out demonic powers, defeated Satan, won the victory over sin, healed sicknesses, conquered death and overcame the forces of nature. These acts were signs of the victory of the kingdom, that God might reign supreme.

The highest summit of kingdom life is that God the Father should be honoured, worshipped and glorified. As we aim for the glories of the kingdom life we shall echo the worship of heaven where 'they fell on their faces before the throne and worshipped God, saying, "Amen! Blessing and glory and wisdom and thanksgiving and honour and power and might be to our God for ever and ever! Amen" (Rev. 7:11–12).

If this little book causes us to fall on our faces before God's throne to worship the Father, then it has played its part in the life of the kingdom.

QUESTIONS FOR DISCUSSION

Chapter 1

1 What does God do for us as our king today?
2 In what way could we be in danger of replacing God's kingship and submitting to human substitutes?
3 List the main point of each of the kingdom parables. How do they apply to us today?

Chapter 2

1 How does the unique kingship of Christ relate to the role of our parents, the government and church leaders?
2 What 'idols' are you tempted to put above Jesus Christ?
3 Discuss the tension between faith in Christ as the all-powerful king and as the meek suffering servant. How does this work out in our Christian life?

Chapter 3

1 What does it mean to be 'born again'? How does Jesus' death on the cross make this possible?
2 Share with others your experience of the reality of new birth.
3 What 'cost' has there been for you in entering the kingdom? How has the Lord compensated you for these sacrifices?

Chapter 4

1 Repentance and righteousness – in practical terms what have these meant for you? How does this affect your life as a member of your church?
2 What are you doing and what could you do to bring greater social justice to your area or country or to the wider world?
3 Discuss the work of God's Spirit in bringing a) peace, b) joy, c) power.
4 What could you do to help in the spread of the gospel to all nations around the world?
5 Are non-Christian religions demonic? Or are they ways to God like Christianity? How do we as Christians view other religions?

Chapter 5

1 Do you tend to overemphasise the present reality of the kingdom?

2 In what ways does our glorious future hope affect our lives today?
3 Are you ‘watching’ and ready for Christ’s coming? If not, why not?
4 What aspects of our future glory thrill you most?

BIBLIOGRAPHY

Easy reading

N. Anderson, *The Teaching of Jesus* (Hodder & Stoughton, 1983)

W. Chantry, *God's Righteous Kingdom* (Banner of Truth, 1980)

A. M. Hunter, *Christ and the Kingdom* (St Andrews Press, 1980)

D. Kraybill, *The Upside-Down Kingdom* (Marshalls, 1985)

M. Lawson, *The Unfolding Kingdom* (Kingsway, 1987)

H. Snyder, *Kingdom Lifestyle* (Marshalls, 1986)

J. Wimber, *Power Evangelism* (Hodder & Stoughton, 1985)

Harder Reading

M. Arias, *Announcing the Reign of God* (Fortress Press, 1984)

G. R. Beasley-Murray, *Jesus and the Kingdom of God* (Paternoster Press/Wm B. Eerdmans, 1986)

E. Castro, *Sent Free* (Wm B. Eerdmans, 1985)
B. Chilton (ed.), *The Kingdom of God* (SPCK, 1984)
G. E. Ladd, *The Gospel of the Kingdom* (Paternoster Press, 1959)
G. E. Ladd, *The Presence of the Future* (SPCK, 1980)
C. G. Montefiore and H. Loewe, *A Rabbinic Anthology* (Schocken Press, 1974)
R. Padilla, *Mission Between the Times* (Wm B. Eerdmans, 1985)
H. Ridderbos, *The Coming of the Kingdom* (Presbyterian & Reformed Publishing Co., 1962)
S. Schechter, *Aspects of Rabbinic Theology* (Schocken Press, 1961)

Books by Martin and Elizabeth Goldsmith

Don't Just Stand There (IVP/STL, 1976)
Finding Your Way (IVP/STL, 1987)
Getting There From Here (MARC/STL, 1986)
God Can Be Trusted (Kingsway/STL, 1984)
Going Places (IVP/STL, 1979)
Islam and Christian Witness (MARC/STL, 1987)
Leviticus-Deuteronomy (Scripture Union, 1981)
Love Your Local Missionary (MARC/STL, 1984)
Marxism (Keston College, 1976)

Other titles in the Foundations series

He Tells Us To Go

Ian Coffey

Ian Coffey sets out to define what evangelism really means: who it is aimed at, what the Bible says, and leaves unsaid. He asks whether this highly emotive and often misunderstood subject is a twentieth-century phenomenon of mass meetings, or a strictly one-to-one affair. *He Tells Us To Go* also discusses the relationship of evangelism to social action, to the ecumenical movement, and to other religions.

Gets to grips with awkward questions. A very helpful little booklet.

He Gives His Word

Ian Barclay

The Bible is the essential basis for Christian belief: it is particularly important to evangelicals. Too many take it for granted, however, and Ian Barclay challenges common assumptions held, and explains what the Bible is all about: its relevance, authorship, interpretations and apparent contradictions. He demonstrates the continuing centrality of the Bible and the fact that it still speaks directly to Christians today.

He Brings Us Together

Clive Calver

He Brings Us Together traces the roots of evangelical belief and practice, sketches a short history of the movement to the present day, and calls for allegiance to the Bible and a commitment to social action and unity. This book is designed to encourage evangelicals to recognise their identity, their distinctiveness and their common ground with one another across the denominational spectrum.

He Guides Us

Jonathan Lamb

He Guides Us affirms that God does guide the lives of individual Christians precisely and effectively. At the heart of the subject of guidance lies the greatest privilege – knowing God.

This book discusses *how* God guides: through the Bible, fellow Christians, circumstances, gifts, prophecy, dreams and visions. It provides valuable help in discerning God's will and identifying his voice.

He Gives Us Signs

Gerald Coates

Does God still heal today? Is his healing power manifested in the physical world (miraculous healing of specific physical ailments) or is it in the spiritual realm (the healing of our relationship with God through Christ)?

Gerald Coates examines the 'signs and wonders' teaching and movement of recent times, describing how his own attitudes have developed during his ministry.